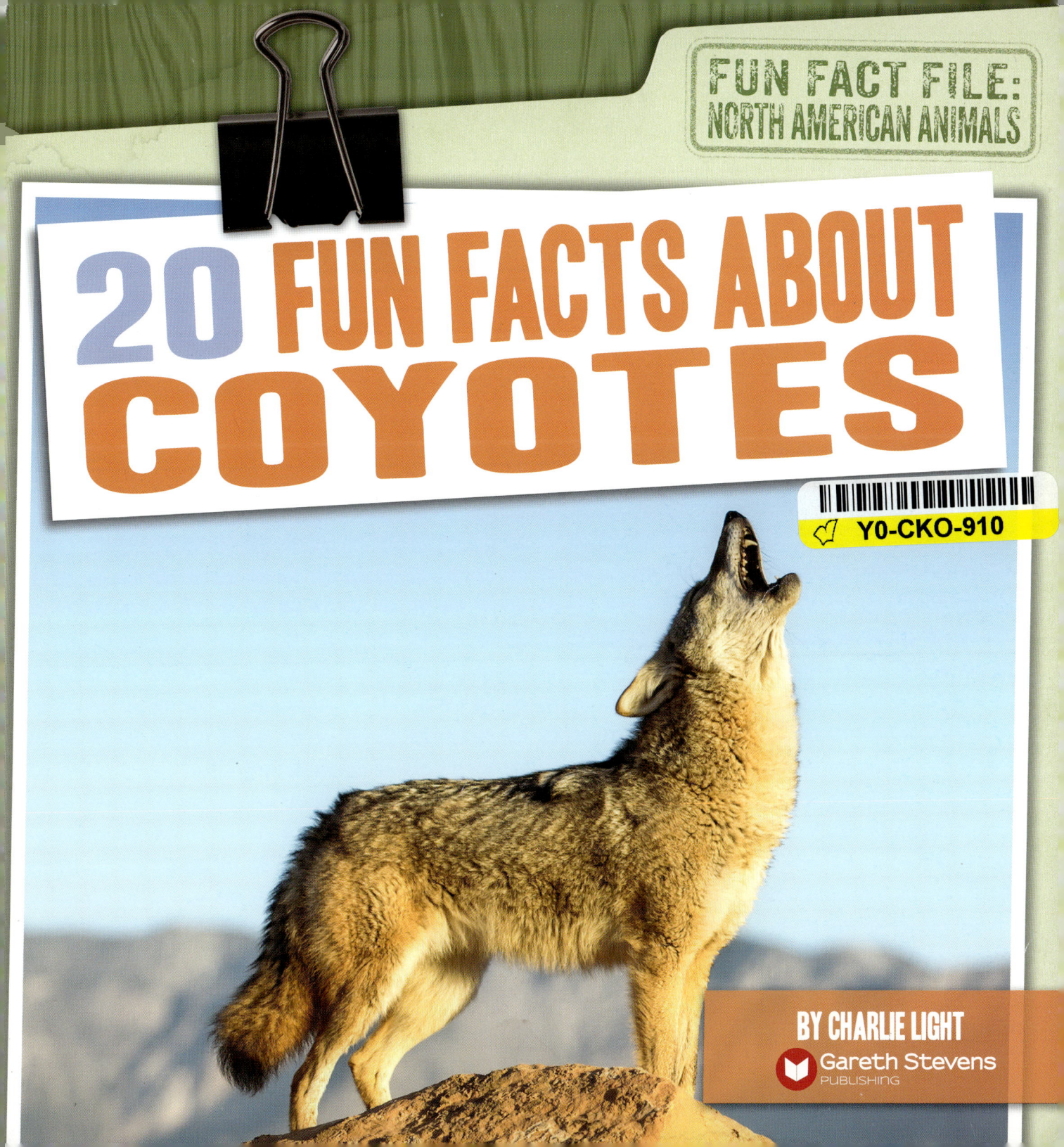

FUN FACT FILE:
NORTH AMERICAN ANIMALS

20 FUN FACTS ABOUT COYOTES

BY CHARLIE LIGHT

Gareth Stevens
PUBLISHING

Please visit our website, www.garethstevens.com. For a free color catalog of all our high-quality books, call toll free 1-800-542-2595 or fax 1-877-542-2596.

To my parents, who gave me binoculars to watch coyotes in my backyard.

Library of Congress Cataloging-in-Publication Data

Names: Light, Charlie, author.
Title: 20 fun facts about coyotes / Charlie Light.
Other titles: Twenty fun facts about coyotes
Description: New York : Gareth Stevens Publishing, [2021] | Series: Fun fact file : North American animals | Includes index.
Identifiers: LCCN 2019049236 | ISBN 9781538257500 (library binding) | ISBN 9781538257487 (paperback) | ISBN 9781538257494 (6 Pack)| ISBN 9781538257517 (ebook)
Subjects: LCSH: Coyote–Juvenile literature.
Classification: LCC QL737.C22 L4927 2021 | DDC 599.77/25–dc23
LC record available at https://lccn.loc.gov/2019049236

First Edition

Published in 2021 by
Gareth Stevens Publishing
111 East 14th Street, Suite 349
New York, NY 10003

Copyright © 2021 Gareth Stevens Publishing

Designer: Sarah Liddell
Editor: Kate Mikoley

Photo credits: Cover, pp. 1 (main), 12 Warren Metcalf/Shutterstock.com; file folder used throughout David Smart/Shutterstock.com; binder clip used throughout luckyraccoon/Shutterstock.com; wood grain background used throughout ARENA Creative/Shutterstock.com; p. 5 JayPierstorff/Shutterstock.com; p. 6 Gleb Tarro/Moment/Getty Images; p. 7 leuntje/Moment Unreleased/Getty Images; p. 8 critterbiz/Shutterstock.com; p. 9 KeithSzafranski/E+/Getty Images; p. 10 Martha Marks/Shutterstock.com; p. 11 Tom Reichner/Shutterstock.com; p. 13 Gerard Garay / 500px/500px/Getty Images; p. 14 Sam Carrera/Shutterstock.com; p. 15 Bruce Gifford/Moment Mobile/Getty Images; p. 16 Kelly vanDellen/Shutterstock.com; p. 17 Amelia Martin/Shutterstock.com; p. 18 Elmar Weiss/500Px Plus/Getty Images; p. 19 James Mattil/Shutterstock.com; p. 20 Guido Vincente Senff/Shutterstock.com; p. 21 Diane079F/Shutterstock.com; p. 22 Jim Cumming/Moment/Getty Images; p. 23 Tom Murphy/National Graphic Image Collection/Getty Images; p. 25 richardseeleyphotography.com/Moment Open/Getty Images; p. 26 Trevor Clark/Shutterstock.com; p. 29 Josef Pittner/Shutterstock.com.

All rights reserved. No part of this book may be reproduced in any form without permission in writing from the publisher, except by a reviewer.

Printed in the United States of America

Some of the images in this book illustrate individuals who are models. The depictions do not imply actual situations or events.

CPSIA compliance information: Batch #CS20GS: For further information contact Gareth Stevens, New York, New York at 1-800-542-2595.

Find us on f ⃝

CONTENTS

Meet the Pack!.....................................4
Master Adapters...................................6
Family Life.......................................8
Mark Your Spot!..................................12
Leave the Pack, Jack!............................14
Not Picky Eaters.................................16
On the Hunt......................................18
Singing Songs....................................22
Won't You Be My Neighbor?........................26
Part of the Pack.................................28
Glossary...30
For More Information.............................31
Index..32

Words in the glossary appear in **bold** type the first time they are used in the text.

MEET THE PACK!

You wake up in the middle of the night. What's that strange, scary sound coming from outside? Is it an alarm? No—it sounds like an animal. Is it a wolf howling? Not quite...it's too high and screechy.

Now there are more animals making the sound. Are the neighborhood dogs all barking together? You creep over to your window and peek into your backyard. Far away, you see them—a pack of coyotes howling under the moon!

Coyotes are famous for their howls, or the long, loud cries they make. They make other unusual noises too.

MASTER ADAPTERS

FUN FACT: 1

COYOTES HAVE ADAPTED TO ENVIRONMENTS RANGING FROM ALASKA TO MEXICO!

Coyotes used to live mainly in the **prairies** and deserts of North America and Mexico. Now, they also live in farmlands, forests, mountains, and even **tropical** environments.

Coyotes can be found in many national parks, such as Yosemite, shown above.

This sign in Vancouver, Canada, tells people to watch out for coyotes. Do you think people in cities can learn to live with their new coyote neighbors safely?

FUN FACT: 2

COYOTES HAVE EVEN MOVED INTO CITIES!

Due to people taking over their natural **habitats**, more coyotes are adapting to life in **urban** environments. You can even spot them in big cities like New York City; Los Angeles, California; and Vancouver, Canada.

FAMILY LIFE

FUN FACT: 3

COYOTES ARE THOUGHT OF AS LONERS, BUT THEY OFTEN LIVE IN PACKS!

The pack is led by an **alpha** female and alpha male pair. They raise their pups, or babies, together. Some pups stay in the pack to help care for the babies to come.

Coyote pups are born in litters. A litter is a group of animals born to the same mother at the same time.

Pups are blind when they're born. In just a few weeks, they're ready to leave the den!

FUN FACT: 4

COYOTES ARE BORN UNDERGROUND!

Coyotes mate, or come together to make babies, between January and March. The female finds a **burrow** dug by other animals or digs her own. She'll give birth to her litter of four to seven pups here.

By making sure there aren't too many coyotes in an area, the coyotes don't have to fight over food.

FUN FACT: 5

COYOTES CAN CONTROL THEIR OWN POPULATIONS!

Scientists have found that female coyotes will have smaller litters when there are a lot of other coyotes in their area and larger litters when there are fewer other coyotes.

FUN FACT: 6

COYOTES CAN MATE WITH DOGS.

The offspring, or babies, of a coyote and a dog are called "coydogs." There aren't many coydogs because the pups are usually born in winter, making it hard for them to live.

Eastern coyotes, such as the one above, are sometimes called coywolves. However, these animals are usually part coyote, wolf, and dog.

MARK YOUR SPOT!

FUN FACT: 7

COYOTES PEE TO MARK WHERE THEY LIVE!

Coyotes are very territorial. This means they guard their territory, or home, from other packs. They pee on their territory to show it belongs to them. They also mark their territory with feces, or poop!

In natural areas, coyote territories are usually between 4 to 15 squares miles (10 to 39 square km).

Although coyotes naturally hunt during the day, they will change when they hunt and are active just to stay away from people! That's why urban coyotes mostly hunt at night.

FUN FACT: 8

URBAN COYOTES CAN MAKE ONE TERRITORY FROM LOTS OF SMALL SPOTS IN NATURE.

Coyotes like big parks and forests away from humans the best. But they're able to live in the pockets of nature in human areas, like soccer fields!

LEAVE THE PACK, JACK!

FUN FACT: 9

SOME COYOTES ARE LONE RANGERS.

This means they don't live with a pack. Coyotes that live alone are called transients. This word means something that stays in a place only for a short time. Coyotes that live in packs are called residents.

Transient coyotes have often just left their parents' pack. They can join a new pack if the alpha pair lets them.

Some transient coyotes are older or sick. They may have been kicked out of their pack.

FUN FACT: 10

MANY TRANSIENT COYOTES LIVE LIFE ON THE ROAD.

Transient coyotes don't have territories the way packs do. Instead, they have a big area of land they move around in. They like to be in places between packs' territories, including areas near roads.

NOT PICKY EATERS

FUN FACT: 11

COYOTES ARE OMNIVORES—THAT MEANS THEY EAT BOTH MEAT AND PLANTS!

Coyotes are known for not being picky about what they eat. They eat many **mammals**, from mice to deer. But they'll also eat snakes, frogs, bugs, dead animals, grass, and fruits.

Coyotes sometimes eat animals that are already dead and rotten, called carrion.

Coyotes are often thought to eat pets like cats and small dogs. While this does happen, it's actually pretty uncommon.

FUN FACT: 12

COYOTES CAN HELP FARMERS!

While coyotes sometimes kill farm animals, they also eat pests, such as mice. Some packs living in areas with sheep even act as guards. By guarding their own territory, they're also guarding the sheep from other, more dangerous coyotes.

ON THE HUNT

FUN FACT: 13

COYOTES GO MOUSING!

When hunting alone, coyotes often stalk, or quietly follow, small **prey** like mice. Then they pounce, or jump suddenly at the prey. This is called mousing—although they also eat lots of other small prey, like rabbits!

Coyotes commonly hunt alone, but they may also hunt in pairs.

Coyotes have a powerful sense of smell. They can smell small mammals like gophers hiding under the snow.

FUN FACT: 14

COYOTES HAVE A TRICK FOR HUNTING UNDER SNOW.

To break through the top layer of harder snow, coyotes stand on their back legs and smash down on the snow with their front paws. This helps them get to softer snow. Now they can dig for the prey!

Coyotes need help from their pack to take down large prey. This one is being chased away by two elk!

FUN FACT: 15

COYOTES WORK TOGETHER TO KILL LARGER PREY, SUCH AS DEER.

They take turns chasing the deer to tire it out. Sometimes, the group will chase the deer toward one hiding coyote. This coyote catches the deer by surprise and attacks it.

FUN FACT: 16

SOMETIMES COYOTES ARE THE ONES BEING HUNTED.

In the wild, coyotes can live six to eight years. They sometimes die from illnesses, but humans also cause many coyote deaths. People kill coyotes by hunting them or by hitting them with cars by mistake.

Humans hunt coyotes for their pelts, or skin and fur, which can be used to make clothes. Some people are against hunting animals for their fur.

SINGING SONGS

FUN FACT: 17

THE LATIN NAME FOR COYOTES, *CANIS LATRANS*, MEANS "BARKING DOG."

Coyotes are named for the strange noises they make. They howl, **growl**, bark, and make high, short noises called "yips." When they string these strange noises together, it can sound like singing!

A scientist found that coyotes make 11 different noises. These noises can mean different things depending on what's going on.

People have learned a lot about how language works by studying coyote noises. What else could we learn from these creatures?

FUN FACT: 18

EACH COYOTE SINGS ITS OWN SONG!

When a lone coyote wants to let its pack know where it is, it lets out a set of barks and then howls. The pack knows who's talking by the sound of the animal's howl!

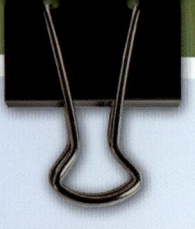

CRACK THE COYOTE CODE

GROWL
"BACK OFF!"

COYOTES MAKE THIS NOISE AS A THREAT, OR A WARNING, TO OTHER ANIMALS.

WHINE
"YOU'RE IN CHARGE!"

THIS NOISE SHOWS THE COYOTE IS SUBMITTING TO, OR BACKING DOWN FROM, ANOTHER COYOTE.

GROUP YIP-HOWL
"WE'RE BACK TOGETHER!" OR "SEE YOU LATER!"

COYOTES MAKE THIS NOISE WHEN THE PACK GETS BACK TOGETHER AFTER BEING APART. THEY ALSO MAKE THIS NOISE AS A GROUP BEFORE THEY SEPARATE TO GO HUNTING ALONE!

WOO-OO-WOW
"HELLO!"

THIS IS AN ENERGETIC COYOTE GREETING.

These are some noises in the coyote code that scientists have cracked!

FUN FACT: 19

COYOTES HAVE A SPECIAL TRICK FOR MAKING THEIR GROUP SEEM LARGER THAN IT IS.

The coyotes howl together, quickly going up and down in pitch. By doing this, two or three coyotes can sound like more than ten coyotes!

These two coyotes can sound like a big pack! This is helpful for scaring away threats—including other packs of coyotes that might be near.

25

WON'T YOU BE MY NEIGHBOR?

FUN FACT: 20

MORE PEOPLE ARE KILLED BY GOLF BALLS THAN ARE BITTEN BY COYOTES EACH YEAR!

Coyotes almost never attack humans. They try their best to stay away from us. Most coyote attacks happen when humans feed them or get very close to them.

If a coyote is hanging around a place with lots of people, like a playground, it might be begging for food. This is when coyotes are dangerous!

HOW CAN WE BE NEIGHBORS?

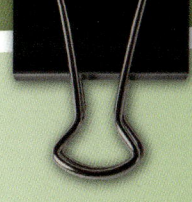

WHAT CAN HUMANS DO?	DOES IT WORK?	WHY?
CATCH COYOTES WITH TRAPS AND MOVE THEM FAR AWAY FROM THEIR URBAN TERRITORY.	NO!	TRAPS OFTEN HURT COYOTES AND OTHER ANIMALS THAT GET CAUGHT IN THEM. EVEN IF THEY'RE MOVED, COYOTES WILL TRY TO GET BACK TO THEIR URBAN TERRITORY.
KILL COYOTES IN URBAN AREAS.	NO!	WHEN HUMANS KILL THE COYOTES IN ONE AREA, NEW COYOTES WILL JUST MOVE IN. MANY PEOPLE ARE AGAINST KILLING COYOTES.
LET COYOTES CONTROL THEIR OWN POPULATION.	YES!	COYOTES ALREADY NATURALLY CONTROL THEIR NUMBERS AND IT'S UNLIKELY THERE WILL EVER BE TOO MANY COYOTES IN A TERRITORY.
BRING PETS AND FOOD INSIDE.	YES!	HUMANS CAN KEEP COYOTES AWAY BY BRINGING THEIR PETS AND FOOD INDOORS AT NIGHT.
NEVER FEED OR GET CLOSE TO COYOTES.	YES!	MOST ATTACKS HAPPEN WHEN HUMANS TRY TO FEED OR TOUCH COYOTES.

Trapping or killing coyotes to get them out of an area doesn't actually lower the number that will live there. If humans remove coyotes, more will move in!

PART OF THE PACK

You've learned so much about your furry neighbors. Now you know that coyotes are an important and interesting part of the environments they live in—even in human habitats! Like many things in nature, coyotes are not usually a danger to humans as long as we give them plenty of space and respect.

Maybe next time you hear them singing outside your window, you can try to decode their songs. See if you can figure out what they may be saying to each other!

Coyotes also use body language, or the way they move or position their bodies, to get their messages across.

29

GLOSSARY

adapt: to change to suit conditions

alpha: an animal that is a leader in its pack

burrow: an underground home dug by an animal

environment: the conditions that surround a living thing and affect the way it lives

growl: to make a deep, often angry, sound

habitat: the natural place where an animal or plant lives

mammal: a warm-blooded animal that has a backbone and hair, breathes air, and feeds milk to its young

prairie: a large, mostly flat area of land in North America covered with grass and very few trees

prey: an animal that is hunted by other animals for food

tropical: having to do with the warm parts of Earth near the equator

urban: having to do with the city

FOR MORE INFORMATION

BOOKS

Avett, Harper. *Coyotes*. New York, NY: PowerKids Press, 2017.

Daniels, Patricia. *Mammals*. Washington, DC: National Geographic Kids, 2019.

McKinnon, Elaine. *Watch Out for Coyotes!* New York, NY: PowerKids Press, 2016.

WEBSITES

Animal Fact Sheet: Coyote
www.desertmuseum.org/kids/oz/long-fact-sheets/coyote.php
Learn more about coyote adaptations and habitats here.

Coyote
kids.nationalgeographic.com/animals/mammals/coyote/
Watch coyote pups at play and learn more about them here!

Urban Coyote Initiative
urbancoyoteinitiative.com/
Learn more about urban coyotes—and how humans can live with them safely—on this site!

Publisher's note to educators and parents: Our editors have carefully reviewed these websites to ensure that they are suitable for students. Many websites change frequently, however, and we cannot guarantee that a site's future contents will continue to meet our high standards of quality and educational value. Be advised that students should be closely supervised whenever they access the internet.

INDEX

alpha 8, 14
attacks 20, 26, 27
body language 29
carrion 16
cars 21
cities 7
coydogs 11
coywolves 11
deer 16, 20
dogs 4, 11, 17, 22
eat 16, 17, 18
environments 6, 7, 28
farmers 17
female 8, 9, 10
fur 21, 28
habitat 7, 28

howls 4, 5, 22, 23, 24, 25
hunting 13, 18, 19, 21
Latin name 22
litter 8, 9, 10
male 8
mousing 18
nature 13, 28
neighbors 7, 28
night 4, 13, 27
omnivores 16
pack 4, 8, 12, 14, 15, 17, 20, 23, 24, 25
parents 14
parks 6, 13
paws 19
people 7, 21, 26, 27
pests 17

populations 10, 27
prey 18, 19, 20
pups 8, 9, 11
residents 14
respect 28
roads 15
scientists 10, 22, 24
sleep 13
smell 19
snow 19
sounds 4, 22, 23, 25
territory 12, 13, 15, 17, 27
threats 24, 25
transients 14, 15
trapping 27